CATHARSIS OF THE SOUL

Staten House

CATHARSIS OF THE SOUL

A Journey Through the Ink

TANIA WINTHER

CATHARSIS OF THE SOUL
Imprint: Staten House
Copyright @2024
2nd edition
Ingramspark publishing
https://atelierwinther.no/my-poetry

A poet sees the world through different eyes
Discovers beauty in unexpected guise
Finds words to express what others feel
and paints with language a picture that's real

Through verse and rhyme
a poet can convey the deepest
thoughts we struggle to say
And touch our souls with a single line
Creating a moment that's truly divine

So let us celebrate the poet's art
And all the ways it touches our heart
For in their words, we find a kind of grace
That lingers with us in time and in space.

Tania Winther

Introduction

In the deepest depths of the human soul lies a profound reservoir of emotions, experiences, and memories. It is a vast landscape where joy, sorrow, love, and pain intertwine, creating many layers that define our unique essence. Within this intricate web of feelings, the concept of catharsis emerges as a powerful force, guiding us through the journey of self-discovery and healing.

Catharsis is the sacred release of pent-up emotions, the purging of emotional burdens that weigh upon the soul. Like a gentle rain washing away the dust of time, catharsis cleanses our inner world, allowing us to confront our deepest fears and vulnerabilities. It is through this process that we begin to unravel the complexities of our emotions, peeling back the layers of our being to uncover the raw essence that lies within.

At times, the soul becomes a vessel that overflows with emotions, struggling to contain the intensity of its experiences. This internal storm can be overwhelming, threatening to drown us in a sea of unexpressed feelings. But catharsis offers a lifeboat, a safe passage through turbulent waters. It invites us to embrace vulnerability and openness, to release the dams that hold back the torrents of emotion.

There are myriad paths to catharsis—art, music, dance, writing, and even sharing heartfelt conversations with kindred spirits. Each of these becomes a medium through which the soul finds its voice. Like an artist wielding a brush on a blank canvas, we paint our emotions onto the world, giving them form and substance. Through this act of creation, we gain clarity and understanding, finding solace in the act of expression.

As we journey deeper into catharsis, we may stumble upon buried wounds and memories that have long been ignored. Though painful, this is a crucial phase of healing. By facing our past with courage, we embrace our humanity and open the door to transformation. The healing process requires patience and gentleness, for catharsis is not a single event but a continuous unfolding of the soul's journey.

In the aftermath of catharsis, we find renewal—a newfound lightness in our steps, a sense of liberation. The weight that once burdened us lifts, and we emerge as if reborn, for catharsis allows us to shed old skins and step into our authenticity. We become more attuned to ourselves and to the world around us, forging deeper connections with others.

In "Catharsis of the Soul," I embark on a deeply introspective journey, delving into the profound aspects of the human experience. My own soul searching led to me rediscovering myself. Through this collection of heartfelt poetry, the book explores loss, grief, heartbreak, and the ever-enigmatic emotion of love. Each piece serves as a poignant tribute to the complexities of life, celebrating both vulnerabilities and strengths.

The poems within this compilation not only delve into the intricacies of love but also lay bare the complexities of the human psyche. With every haiku, unsent love letter, and serenade, I unravel the essence of loss, unhealthy love and heartbreak, inviting you to resonate with these raw and authentic emotions.

As you delve into the pages of "Catharsis of the Soul," you are encouraged to embrace your own vulnerabilities and find solace in the transformative power of resilience. This book serves as a mirror reflecting the nature of our existence, encouraging us to confront our imperfections and find strength in the stories of triumph and tribulation.

I hope that "Catharsis of the Soul" allows you to accept yourself in the tender intricacies of the heart. Finding comfort and healing within the embrace of shared emotions. Whether it be heartache or love, this anthology unveils the timeless beauty of our collective human experiences.

With all my love,
Tania

Oh, how the world around us fades away
As we gaze deeply into each other's eyes
And all our fears and worries disappear
In this moment of pure love and sweet surprise.

The Writer

I write of love, of pain, of joy
Of all the things that life employs
My words are my window to the world
A lens through which my thoughts unfurl

As a writer, I am both observer and participant
A witness to life's beauty and its torment
I capture the essence of the human condition
And translate it into words with precision

Sometimes my writing is met with praise
Other times, it's met with a critical gaze
But I write on, undaunted by the critics' sting
For in my heart, I know the power that words can bring

For words have the power to heal and to mend
To lift up broken hearts and help them transcend
And in this way, I am honored to be a writer
To share my stories and make the world a little brighter

So let me continue to write and to create
To mold my words into a beautiful swirl of fate
And let them flow from my heart and my soul
To touch the hearts of many, and make them whole.

HEARTBREAK

Torn pages of love
Unwritten chapters of dreams
Heartbreak's legacy.

Heartbreak

In the deep void of sorrow, where shadows lie
Comes a tale of heartbreak, a tearful sigh
A tender heart shattered, love's fragile thread
Aching with longing, words left unsaid

A love once cherished, now torn apart
Leaving behind a wounded heart
Promises whispered, like gentle breeze
Now broken fragments, memories that freeze

The world loses color, turns shades of gray
As sadness envelops, clouding the way
Each beat of the heart echoes with pain
A haunting melody, a mournful refrain

The days grow heavy, nights filled with tears
Echoes of laughter, fading with the years
The emptiness lingers, a vacant space
Aching reminders of a lost embrace

But through the darkness, hope's flickering light
Whispers of healing in the depths of night
For hearts can mend, though scars remain
And love can bloom, after the rain

Take solace in time, the mender of souls
Allowing wounds to heal, making them whole
Embrace the lessons learned, the strength you'll find
To love again, leaving heartbreak behind.

Love Letters
Unsent

My Dearest

As I sit here, penning these words, my heart aches with a profound sadness that I can scarcely put into words. It feels as though a tempest of emotions is raging within me, and the weight of our shattered love bears down upon my soul.

I remember the day we first met, how our eyes locked in an instant, and I knew deep within me that you were the missing piece of my puzzle. From that moment on, my love for you grew with an intensity that I never thought possible. You became the sun that illuminated my darkest days, the soothing balm to my deepest wounds.

But alas, it seems our love has become entangled in the thorny vines of circumstance and misunderstanding. The once vibrant bond we shared has withered away, leaving behind only fragments of what was once a beautiful tapestry of affection. It pains me to witness the unraveling of our love, as if watching a rose slowly wilt and lose its petals, until all that remains is a faded memory of what once bloomed so brilliantly.

I replay our moments together in my mind, the laughter, the whispered promises, and the shared dreams. Each memory now carries a bittersweet tinge, for they are no longer the foundation upon which our future is built. Instead, they serve as painful reminders of a love that now lies in ruins.

I find myself yearning for your touch, for the warmth of your embrace that used to chase away all my fears. I miss the way your eyes sparkled with affection when you looked at me, as if I were the center of your universe. But now, I am left with a void in my heart that no amount of tears can fill.

Though I know it is time to let go, it doesn't make the act any easier. My heart longs for a love that can no longer be, and it feels as though a piece of my very essence has been torn away. But I must find the strength to heal and move forward, even if it feels impossible right now.

Know that I will forever cherish the love we once shared, even though it now resides in the realm of memories. I will carry the lessons learned from our time together, and I will strive to become a better person because of the love we once knew. Wishing you nothing but happiness, my dear, even if it's not with me.

May life bestow upon you all the love and joy you deserve. With a broken heart and bittersweet memories,

Yours truly ...

My Beloved

As I gather the courage to write this letter, memories of our time together flood my mind, and I am reminded of the profound impact you had on my understanding of love. You became my guide, unveiling the intricacies of Greek love: Eros, Philia, Agape, and Storge – each a unique form of love.

Eros, the passionate and romantic love, was the spark that ignited the flames of desire between us. Our hearts danced to the rhythm of its intensity, as we reveled in the intoxicating allure of each other's presence. The enchantment of Eros bound us together, and the moments we shared were like fragments of a timeless love story.

Philia, the love of friendship, was the sturdy foundation upon which our connection was built. In the laughter we shared and the secrets we confided, I found a companion in you – someone who understood me beyond words, and whose presence brought comfort and joy to my life.

Agape, the selfless and unconditional love, transcended the boundaries of the physical realm. It was a love that embraced flaws, celebrated strengths, and cherished every moment we spent together. In your unwavering support and care, I felt a love that gave without asking for anything in return, and that remains etched in my heart.

And then there was Storge, the love of family and familiarity. Our journey allowed us to become intertwined in each other's lives, creating bonds that mirrored those of kinship. The warmth of Storge fostered a sense of belonging, and I felt a sense of home in your arms, a sanctuary where I could be vulnerable and true. With your guidance, I came to recognize the profound depth of these four loves in our relationship. Each one colored our story in a unique hue, creating a canvas of emotions that made us both vulnerable and resilient. But even with this newfound wisdom, questions gnaw at my soul, wondering if I truly understood the magnitude of your love, or if I failed to grasp its entirety.

I question myself, asking if I was enough for you, or if my expectations were too lofty. Perhaps my grasp of love's intricacies was not as profound as yours, leading us to drift apart in the ebb and flow of emotions.

Despite the uncertainty and heartache, I choose to remember the beautiful moments we shared – the laughter, the tears, and the unspoken words that resonated between us. You will always occupy a special place in my heart, and I am grateful for the love you taught me in its many forms.

As I write these words, I wish you happiness and contentment on your journey through life. May you continue to explore the depths of love and find the solace and companionship you seek. As for me, I will hold onto the memories and lessons you gifted me, embracing the complexity of love and cherishing its presence in all its forms.

With a heart that once belonged to you,

Yours ...

My Love

As I gather the courage to write this letter, memories of our time I find myself at a loss for words as I attempt to articulate the anguish that consumes my every waking moment. It is a pain that is born from the realization that the love we once held so dearly has fractured beyond repair, leaving me in a state of perpetual heartache.

When we first embarked on this journey together, I never fathomed that it would end in such devastation. I believed, with every fiber of my being, that our love was unbreakable, a force that could weather any storm. But life had other plans for us, and now I am left picking up the shattered fragments of a love that once felt indestructible.

It feels as though my heart is caught in a relentless tempest, tossed and turned by waves of sorrow and regret. The memories of our time together haunt me, the sweetness of your touch and the tenderness in your eyes now twisted into painful reminders of what we have lost. How could something so beautiful crumble into ruins?

I find myself retracing our steps, analyzing every word spoken and every action taken, desperately searching for the moment when it all began to unravel. But in the end, it matters little where the fault lies. The truth is, we have grown apart, our paths diverging into separate journeys that we must now undertake alone.

Yet, even in the midst of this heartbreak, I want you to know that my love for you remains. It is a love that will forever be etched upon my soul, despite the pain it now inflicts. You were my everything, my reason for believing in the power of love, and even as I nurse the wounds of our parting, I cannot deny the impact you had on my life.

As I bid you farewell, I do so with a mix of sadness and hope. Sadness for the love we lost, but hope for the love that awaits us both. May you find happiness in the arms of another, someone who will cherish you as deeply as I once did. And may the pain of our parting transform into a lesson that guides us towards greater self-discovery and a love that will never falter.

With a heart burdened by the weight of goodbye,

Yours truly ...

*Four Types
of Love*

Eros

Eros, the flame that set our hearts alight
Passion's touch, igniting day and night
In your embrace, desires found their peak
A love so fierce, we dared not speak.

Philia

Philia, the bond of friendship's grace
In laughter, secrets, we found our place
A friend in you, a soul that understood
Beyond mere words, a friendship made of good.

Agape

Agape, a love so selfless and pure
In your support, I found a love secure
Accepting flaws, and strengths alike
A love that asked for naught in its delight.

Storge

Storge, the love of kinship and embrace
A sense of home, a familial space
Our lives entwined, in rope of ties
A sanctuary found in each other's eyes.

Questions lingered in the depths of me
Did I comprehend love's vast decree?
Why was I not enough, my dear?
Did I misread the love I held so near?

But through it all, I choose to hold
The memories that our love once told
In moments shared, our souls were bared
A journey of love, both brave and scared

Farewell, my love, with heart once thine
I'll cherish our love's past and shine
In your absence, I'll grow anew
Embracing love in all its forms, so true.

In love's bitter wake
Whispers of what could have been
Fading echoes ache.

MEMORIES

I sometimes get lost in my memories
It is like I am stuck in time
Are they true
Or are they just fragments of pieces
I am still here
It's time to move on.

Lust

His touch, a brush of fire on my skin
Awakens senses, ignites the fire within
Soft whispers of longing, a lover's plea
His breath, a gentle breeze, setting me free

In the tender darkness, our souls unite
Exploring each other, like stars in the night
Fingers tracing secrets, seeking divine
The rhythm of Eros, our hearts intertwine

His lips, like nectar, sweet and divine
A taste of heaven, a love so fine
Weaving dreams, as we move in sync
In the poetry of passion, we eternally link

In the embrace of Eros, we find release
A sanctuary of love, a sacred peace
Desires unlocked, as bodies entwine
In this dance of love, our souls align

He's my Adonis, a god to adore
Our love story writ on a celestial floor
With every caress, a new verse we write
In the tender arms of Eros' delight

Time suspends, as ecstasy unfolds
In the temple of love, our story's told
In the depths of passion, we find our home
Bound by Eros, forever we'll roam.

Guarding Faded Memories

In solitude, where echoes softly roam
Stands a house in stillness, where hearts once found a home
The door now closed, a silent sentinel it seems
Guarding memories faded, like whispers in our dreams

Once, laughter danced upon these floors of polished grace
Love painted every corner, filling up the empty space
But time, that unyielding force, wove tales of change and woe
Leaving behind a vacant shell, where shadows come and go

The door closed, a threshold crossed, no footfalls mark the ground
No voices fill the chambers, nor laughter can be found
The portraits on the walls, their eyes devoid of life
Tell stories of departed souls, a longing for their strife

In empty halls, a song of silence slowly plays
Resonating through the rooms, in melancholic haze
The memories now fragile, like whispers on the breeze
Whispered secrets fade away, as the heartache starts to ease

But amidst the vacant rooms, a subtle flicker gleams
A hint of whispered hope, like echoes of lost dreams
For though the house may stand alone, its heart forever beats.

A hiatus, a break in time
A pause that halts the daily grind
A moment to breathe, to rest and reflect
To gather strength and self-respect.

Love's Serenade

In twilight's embrace, beneath the starry skies
My heart yearns for you, love that never dies
Yet fate has laced a arras of pain
Two worlds apart, our love shall remain

Oh, my love, hear my voice on the breeze
Whispering secrets through the distant trees
Though oceans divide us, and worlds set us apart
Know that you reside forever in my heart

In dreams, I reach out, fingers graze the moon
Longing to be with you, to hold you soon
But reality beckons, its grip so severe
Two souls entwined, yet fate we cannot steer

Oh, my love, hear my voice on the breeze
Whispering secrets through the distant trees
Though oceans divide us, and worlds set us apart
Know that you reside forever in my heart

The sun rises, casting a golden hue
Painting a portrait of love so true
Yet with each dawn, our paths diverge
Two lives entangled, forbidden to merge

In silence, I cherish the memories we've made
Moments frozen in time, a serenade
Though miles may separate us, love transcends
A flame that burns bright, forever it contends

Oh, my love, hear my voice on the breeze
Whispering secrets through the distant trees
Though oceans divide us, and worlds set us apart
Know that you reside forever in my heart

So, I'll carry our love, a treasure untold
A melody of emotions, never growing old
Though destiny may dictate our separate ways
I'll love you fiercely, till the end of my days.

A hiatus, a gift of time
To embrace the present, and make it sublime
To cherish every moment that is bestowed
To find true happiness in the simple and slow

So if life gets too busy and fast
And you need a break to make it last
Remember that a hiatus is not a waste
But a chance to find your inner grace.

UNHEALTHY
LOVE

Love's Illusion

Under the spell of love's illusion, I once believed
In a man who vowed to cherish, never to deceive
But alas, his heart wandered, led astray
Leaving me shattered, in disarray

His words were sweet, a honeyed melody
Yet behind his eyes, a treacherous melody
In the shadows, he danced with deceit
Leaving my heart in fragments, incomplete

Oh, the pain of a love betrayed
A symphony of heartache, never to fade
His unfaithful touch stained my very core
Leaving me breathless, longing for more

I gave him my trust, an offering so pure
Only to discover his love was not secure
In the realm of infidelity, he chose to reside
Leaving my soul bruised, wounded inside

But I shall rise, like a phoenix from the flame
Reclaiming my strength, shedding the blame
For I deserve a love that is true
A love that will never leave my heart askew

So farewell, deceitful lover of mine
Your unfaithful actions, now left behind
I'll mend the pieces of my broken heart
And in time, a new love will impart

For I am resilient, stronger than before
No longer confined by your unfaithful lore
I'll find a love that will stay by my side
A love that will mend the wounds you tried to hide

And in that love, I'll heal and grow
Leaving behind the pain you bestowed
For the scars you left shall fade away
And a love that's faithful will forever stay.

Love's Entrapment

Unhealthy love, a poison within
A trap that ensnares us deep within
A love that's filled with jealousy and fear
That leaves us broken, shedding many a tear

It starts off sweet, like honey on the tongue
But soon it sours, leaving us undone
It's possessive and controlling, a suffocating embrace
Leaving us feeling trapped and out of place

It's a love that's filled with lies and deceit
A love that's never truly complete
It's a love that drains us of our soul
And leaves us feeling empty, a gaping hole

Unhealthy love, it takes and takes
Leaves us with nothing but heartaches
It's a love that we should never seek
For it only leaves us feeling weak

We must learn to recognize the signs
And free ourselves from these love's binds
For love should be a pure and wholesome thing
A love that lifts us up, and makes our hearts sing.

Twisted hearts entwined
Obsession's grip tightens fast
Toxic love devours.

Shattered Dreams

In shattered dreams, I stand alone
A witness to a love that was never truly known
You, the master of deception, played your part
Leaving my fragile heart torn apart

I believed in the promises whispered in the night
But behind closed doors, your infidelity took flight
In the embrace of another, you found delight
While I drowned in a sea of endless plight

Oh, the ache of a heart betrayed
A symphony of tears, forever replayed
You painted a picture of love so divine
Yet behind the facade, a heart so malign

I offered you my trust, my vulnerability laid bare
But you cast it aside without a second thought or care
Your betrayal left wounds that time may heal
But the scars remain, a reminder of what was real

But hear me now, as I reclaim my worth
For I am more than the pain you unearthed
I will mend my broken wings and learn to fly
Far away from your deceitful lies

In the wake of this heartache, I find my voice
A declaration of strength, a resounding choice
I deserve a love that's faithful and true
One that cherishes and honors the love we grew

So farewell to the pain you brought my way
I'll rise above and find a brighter day
For within me burns a resilient flame
Ready to love again, but never the same

I release you now, with a heart set free
Knowing that I deserve a love that will be
True, honest, and steadfast through all
Leaving behind the shadows of your unfaithful fall

And in the echoes of goodbye, I'll find my grace
Embracing a love that's genuine, a warm embrace
For a broken heart can heal and find a new start
In the arms of a love that will never break me apart.

Fractured pieces ache
Heartbreak's symphony of pain
Strength rises from scars.

Survivor

I begged for help. But no one listened
I said we were in danger, but no one believed me and I became even
more like a stranger
I gathered proof, but the proof was deleted
I ended up in silence, because silence felt safer, but it made me
more lonely, and I isolated myself from people
I was completely alone in the dark
No one understood. No one saw
I ran away
Tried to escape
Took jobs far away. but there was no
escape
I was told I was depressed. I had all the symptoms
I was told I was lazy
They told me I was giving up
I survived the abuse, I survived from my grief, I survived losing you
I'm a chameleon trying to adapt
I feel separated from the herd, corralled by my loss and bereavement
My grief is different
My process is complicated
Let me cope my way.

I was drowning
You swallowed me whole
I just didn't notice
I lost sight of who I am
Then I lost it all
I fell into a black hole
And finally I saw myself.

Trauma

Painting is for pictures
hard to understand
so let me paint you a picture in words at hand
There once was a girl who had a little too much to understand
Her heart was a two ton brick in her fist, that kept her dished
It's strange how just a few short seconds can lead you in a whole new
direction. It alters how you think and act, and how you see your own
reflection. From a single moment on, my life was forever changed
Like everything I previously knew had suddenly been rearranged

No one will ever understand just how I felt that day
But deep within this poem I shall try to convey
I cannot even begin to illustrate the repulsive person I once knew
I intend to simply express the horror that I went through
Sometimes late at night I simply can't fall asleep
Thinking about what cannot be undone, rewinds as a nightmare
It is my gruesome reality, that I cannot deny, nor is beyond repair

Behind my smiles and heartfelt kindness I try to extend and express to
you all, it truly does come with sincerity and honesty, but that all too
came with a cost. It has felt the worst of pains and experienced the
greatest loss. I cannot change the past, an event to which I succumbed
But I can focus on the present and change what is to come

We are all so different and yet so much the same
Everyone, in some way or another, will experience a kind of pain
Everybody has things they wish not to recall
Into each life some rain must fall

The trauma of abuse is never fully gone from my consciousness
Its filthy stain leaves its residue on my soul forever.

Bitter love's embrace
Chains of longing and despair
Souls consumed by pain.

The Wounds Will Slowly Mend

In the echoes of a love now lost
I find myself paying the heavy cost
Deceived by lies, betrayed and torn
Yet still, the memories are reborn

The heartbreak lingers, a haunting pain
An emotional storm that won't wane
Deception's dance, a cruel charade
In the wreckage of love, I'm left dismayed

You played mind tricks, a master of disguise
With each illusion, a piece of me dies
But amid the ruins of what we were
The embers of love still softly stir

How can I miss us, you might ask
When you were the architect of this heart's impasse?
Yet love, a complex and mysterious art
Binds us to moments, etched in the heart

In vulnerability, I opened wide
Believed in your love, side by side
But shadows crept into our embrace
And the trust we shared began to efface

Though the pain persists, I must confess
That remnants of love persist no less
The memories of laughter, tender touch
Still haunt my thoughts, I miss them so much

It's not your betrayal that I yearn
But the love we shared, the lessons learned
In letting go, I find release
To heal this heart, to find my peace

In time, the wounds will slowly mend
And I'll emerge, stronger in the end
For love is not bound to just one face
But blooms anew, in a different space

So though the heartbreak holds me tight
I'll rise above the darkest night
And learn to cherish what remains
While freeing myself from binding chains

I'll walk away, my head held high
No longer haunted by your lies
And in the healing, I'll rediscover
A love that's true, a love that's stronger.

Through heart's broken shards
Hope finds a way to mend wounds
Love's light still shines bright.

It seemed I had to reach the bottomless pit of darkness
To understand I had to change my ways
It is time for me to look inwards and nurture myself
It is time for me to find love for myself
And start anew.

GRIEF

Shattered love's debris
Heartache echoes through my soul
Mending, I find peace.

Contrived

There are whispers in the dark. Did you hear them?
They are weeping in perpetual darkness
Like tormented souls in deep sorrow
Like eternal screams and soundless echoes of the past they crucify
the night
I think of freedom in my thoughts
but my thoughts never free me
I try to envision the sky, Green leaves
The past before all pain came our way ...
I closed my eyes, but life imprisoned me
I chose to be quiet. I chose to be unheard. Yet, I was seen as I screamed
in silence
So cry, cry hard, cry deep
Cry because water is life-giving
Cry because you dare
Cry because you can, my dear
There is no escape.

Loss

Losing a child, a pain so deep
A wound that never seems to heal or sleep
A life cut short, a dream undone
Leaving parents with grief that weighs a ton

Memories flash by, of laughter and joy
Of playing together, when they were a girl or a boy
Of watching them grow, and learn to explore
Of the love they gave, and the love they drew

The future imagined, with hopes and plans
Now shattered by fate's cold hands
The emptiness left, a void that's vast
A heart that's broken, shattered at last

The world goes on, but for you, it's still
A moment frozen in time, a void to fill
A life forever changed, a scar to bear
A loss that's felt, beyond compare

May love and memories bring you peace
May time bring a balm to this grief
May your child's light shine on in your heart
As you carry on, never to be apart.

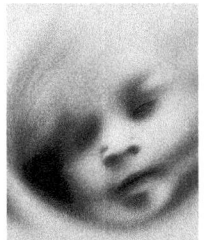

Once cocooned in all my love
You are still with me just flying high above
You're free to let go my darling child
Know that you are eternally loved.

In the Deepest Sorrow

In the depths of sorrow and despair
When loss and grief feel too much to bear
We find ourselves adrift, alone
In a sea of pain we can't disown

We long for what was once so dear
And mourn the love that's no longer here
Our hearts are shattered, and our souls
Are left to wander through these holes

We ask ourselves, why must we endure
The pain that seems so harsh and pure
Why must we face this endless ache
That seems to never give us a break?

But in the midst of all our tears
We find that love still perseveres
For though the ones we've lost are gone
Their memory and spirit will live on

Their presence lingers in our heart
A flame that will never depart
And though their physical form may be gone
Their love and light will always shine on

Let us hold on to the love we've known
And carry it with us as we've grown
For though we may grieve and feel the loss
Their love will always be our guiding force.

In the depths of loss
Heartache reveals hidden strength
Renewal emerges.

Bereavement

When death comes knocking at our door
And takes a loved one we adore
We're left to mourn and to grieve
And wonder how we'll ever believe

That life will go on without them here
That we'll be able to face our fear
Of living in a world that's changed
And learning to cope with the pain

The tears we shed are like a river
That flows on and on forever
They're a testament to our love
And a tribute to the one above

Who holds us close in times of need
And helps us through our darkest deeds
For though our hearts may be broken
Our spirit will never be stolen

We'll keep our memories close at hand
And cherish the moments we had planned
For they will live on in our hearts
Even when we're worlds apart.

Unappreciated

Taken for Granted

In a world where giving flows freely
I offered my heart, sincerely
But in return, I received so little
Feelings taken for granted, a bitter pill

Like a wellspring, I shared my love
Hoping for reciprocation from above
But my efforts were met with apathy
Leaving me lost in a sea of melancholy

I gave my time, my trust, my care
Yet it seemed as if no one was aware
The depth of my emotions, often unseen
Leaving me questioning what it all could mean

But I've learned a valuable lesson here
To cherish my worth, without any fear
For in giving too much, I lost a part of me
But now I reclaim it, setting my spirit free

No longer will I be taken for granted
My heart's treasures now more guarded
I'll find those who appreciate my soul
And together, we'll build a love that's whole.

Selfless acts of care
Taken for granted, unseen
Heart's giving ignored.

A Selfless Heart

In the gift of giving, I extend my hand
Helping others, with intentions grand
But as time passes, a pattern unfolds
Some take and take, their gratitude untold

A selfless heart, I offer my aid
But it seems some souls have a different trade
They receive without pause, without a thought
Leaving me wondering, is my effort for naught?

Yet still, I continue to lend my care
Knowing deep inside why I'm truly there
For in the act of giving, my spirit finds peace
Even if some take more than they release

Though some may exploit, my faith won't sway
In the potential for good, day after day
For even amidst those who only receive
I hold on to hope, and my heart won't grieve

For the joy of helping outweighs the toll
And the impact of kindness can mend the soul
So I'll keep offering my hand to those in need
Knowing that my actions, in essence, succeed.

Endless help extended
Gratitude left unspoken
Unseen kindness fades.

Without Return

In a world where some take without return
I find solace in the lessons I discern
For in giving, I find strength and grace
Even if gratitude seems out of place

I choose to see the impact I make
In hearts touched, even if they don't partake
For true giving is not measured in gain
But in the ripple effect, like a gentle rain

Though some may take and never repay
I'll continue to give, come what may
For in each act of kindness, a seed is sown
That may bloom in ways I've never known

So I'll keep extending my hand, my heart
Knowing that my generosity is an art
For in helping others, I find my own light
A beacon of hope, burning strong and bright.

Unseen hands reach out
Kindness offered, taken for granted
Heart's whispers unheard.

Ebb and Flow

In this vast world of ebb and flow
Some hearts give freely, letting love grow
Their generosity, like a gentle stream
Flows unceasingly, a beautiful theme

But amidst the beauty, some hearts just take
Absorbing energy, causing hearts to ache
They snatch and grasp, with selfish might
Leaving givers weary, depleted from the fight

Why do some souls give endlessly
While others take with such audacity?
Is it the way they're made, their inner core
Or life's lessons they choose to ignore?

The givers thrive on spreading light
In acts of kindness, they find their might
Their joy is found in lifting others high
Bringing smiles and tears of purest sky

Yet the takers, they see only their needs
Unaware of the wounds their taking breeds
Blinded by self-interest, they miss the sight
Of the beauty that blossoms in giving's pure light

But still, the givers continue to impart
Their love, compassion, and a caring heart
For they understand the power they possess
To inspire, uplift, and heal the distressed

Let us celebrate the givers, their selfless grace
Their presence in this world, like a warm embrace
And may we guide the takers, help them see
The joy in giving, setting their spirits free

For in the balance of giving and taking
We find the true essence of a life worth making
Let empathy guide us, as we learn and grow
Creating a world where love's currents freely flow.

Generosity flows
Unseen, unacknowledged acts
Heart's grace still shines bright.

In the cycle of giving, I remain steadfast
Though some take without gratitude's contrast
For in each act of kindness, my purpose is clear
To bring light to their lives, and banish their fear

I may encounter takers on this giving quest
But their actions won't deter me from doing my best
For I've learned that true fulfillment is found
In the act of giving, in love that abounds.

Buried Beneath a Façade

In the deepest of my soul, music plays
A dance of emotions, in curious ways
But amidst the cacophony, a truth I perceive
Feelings contrived, like masks they deceive

Oh, how they twirl and twist, in an intricate display
Painting illusions, leading hearts astray
They masquerade as genuine, wearing their disguise
Yet deep within, a hollow echo lies

A smile that conceals a river of tears
Laughter that masks unresolved fears
Behind the curtain of contrived delight
Lies a yearning for authenticity's light

But why do we construct this elaborate charade
Burying our truth beneath a façade?
Is it the fear of vulnerability's touch
That compels us to contrive, to appear as such?

Yet, in the artifice, a longing resides
To be seen and accepted, where honesty abides
For beneath the layers, a genuine core
Aching to break free, to be embraced once more.

Honor our emotions true
Embrace the rawness, the shades of every hue
For it is in the genuine, the uncontrived art
That we discover the beauty of the human heart.

Shattered love's debris
Heartache echoes through my soul
Mending, I find peace.

A Lesson on Judgement

In ancient times, a tale unfolds
Of a maiden with tresses, so I am told
Born of beauty, a mortal fair
A maiden named Medusa, beyond compare

Her flowing locks, like midnight's shroud
Were once admired by the joyful crowd
But alas, envy took its toll
And turned her fate to something bold

Athena, the goddess of wisdom and grace
Cast her eyes upon Medusa's face
Enraged by her beauty, a curse was cast
Transforming her visage, a spell so vast

Her golden hair turned to serpents' hiss
A fearsome sight, one couldn't dismiss
Her gaze, once tender, now brought despair
For any who met it, turned to stone, so rare

Banished to a desolate island afar
Medusa roamed, a creature bizarre
Her heart, once pure, now filled with sorrow
Her life forever changed, no bright tomorrow

Yet, beneath her monstrous guise
A spirit remained, seeking solace and skies
She yearned for freedom, release from her plight
To find redemption, to see the light

Heroes ventured to face her dread
To sever the snakes, strike her head
And in the end, it came to pass
Perseus, the valiant, a daring task

Medusa's fate, a tragic plight
A reminder of jealousy's might
A symbol of beauty turned awry
Her true essence concealed, by and by

Remember, dear souls, as tales are told
That judgment can turn hearts so cold
For Medusa was more than just a curse
Once a maiden of beauty, before things turned worse.

Letting Go

Ink Spills Like Tears

Ink becomes the brush, the artful key
To cleanse the past, to set me free
With every stroke, a memory fades
A healing journey, the soul cascades

In swirling lines, emotions flow
Unraveling tales, both high and low
The burdened heart finds solace, peace
As past and present gently cease

The words converge, a sacred dance
On parchment's canvas, I enhance
The pain, the joy, the dreams, the strife
Transformed by ink, the trials of life

Through every verse, a weight is lifted
The chains of yesterday, gifted
I pour my heart, my soul, my mind
To find the gems of self, refined

Ink spills like tears, each drop a gem
An alchemy of pain and them
Transforming sorrow into grace
Through ink's embrace, I find my place

The scars upon my heart, they mend
Through verses penned, my soul I tend
Ink bleeds forgiveness, washing clean
The shadows cast by what has been

I lay my past upon the page
Inscribed in ink, a pilgrimage
Through letters formed, I'm free at last
No longer bound by shadows cast

With every stroke, I'm unconfined,
A clutter of self designed
Through ink's catharsis, I transcend
A tale of healing, love, and mend

And as I write, my spirit soars
In ink's embrace, my heart restores
Cleansed and renewed, I boldly stand
Embracing life anew and grand.

Silent tears cascade
Heartbreak's ache within my chest
Healing whispers time.

Tears and Transcendence

In her realm, where teardrops gleam
A twinkling tale of hearts agleam
They tumble down like silver streams
A dance of sorrow, hopes, and dreams

Their shimmer holds a deeper glance
A pathway to the soul's expanse
In her realm, tears lead the dance
A bridge between life's song and trance

Through sorrow's veil, a strength does grow
Transcending realms, a heart may know
In her tears, a story's flow
A journey to a brighter glow

So don't restrain those tears that fall
They echo in her sweet call
Through ups and downs, we stand tall
In tears, we find our way through all

With her grace, we find release
And soar beyond life's burdens' crease
In her realm, our hearts find peace
As tears become our path to bliss.

Did you know butterflies rest when it rains
because it damages their wings?
It's okay to rest during the storms of life
You'll always fly again once it's over.

Trust the process.

Words by: uknown

CATHARSIS

Then Comes Catharsis

In the depths of the soul, a tempest roars
A song of emotions, seeking shores
The burdens of the heart, too heavy to bear
Yearning for release, for solace, for repair

Then comes catharsis, a cleansing rain
Washing over the soul's terrain
A sacred dance of tears and grace
A healing balm for wounds to face

Through ink and canvas, the soul takes flight
Painting its essence, colors bright
Words become wings, soaring high
Unveiling truths, no longer shy

In melodies and rhythms, the heart finds ease
Music's embrace, a sweet release
The soul's whispers, harmonies unfold
A swarm of healing, stories unfold

In the dance's sway, the soul unwinds
Body and spirit, together aligned
Embracing movements, free and wild
A dance of catharsis, undefiled

Through laughter's embrace, the spirit lifts
A burst of joy, a soul's sweet gift
With every giggle, lightness found
In shared delight, hearts are bound

Catharsis, the key to soul's reprise
A journey deep, where healing lies
In vulnerability, strength is found
A phoenix rising from the ground

So let the soul embrace the gale
Through tears and laughter, it shall prevail
For catharsis brings the soul to whole
An alloy of healing, a song of the soul.

Wounds of love run deep
Embracing shadows of pain
Healing starts to seep.

Into the Void

In the void of unknown, my spirit was lost
A journey through shadows, a chilling frost
Yet from the abyss, I emerged to the light
A riddle unraveling, a celestial flight

In death's embrace, my essence did fade
But a cosmic puzzle, my fate remade
In waking again, I beheld a new start
A conundrum of life, a key to my heart

In the concept of time, I once was confined
Yet my riddle's answer, I now shall find
For in the mysteries, I rediscover
All the enchanting joys of life's cover

I missed the stars' dance, the moon's sweet song
That of nature, where I belong
Now I seize the day, embrace every gleam
In the riddle's solution, I dare to dream

With each breath, I embark on this quest
A rhythm of wonders, my heart's request
In the rhyme of existence
I'll forge my path with steadfast persistence

No longer lost in the void's embrace
I roam the universe, with newfound grace
My riddle of life, I'll unravel
As I chase my dreams, and my spirit retrieve.

Whispers of goodbye
Heartbreak's bittersweet refrain
New beginnings bloom.

Every Friday

Every Friday, a gift so sweet
Flowers from my ex, a gesture complete
Petals of love, vibrant and bright
A tradition that brought joy and delight

Once we were entwined, love's gentle bloom
But now we've moved on, to different rooms
Yet the memories linger, in petals arrayed
A reminder of love that once brightly swayed

Now it's my turn, the torch I bear
To continue this tradition, show that I care
I've taken the responsibility, embraced it whole
To bring beauty and joy, to my heart and soul

With every Friday's dawn, I seek out a bloom
A fragrant reminder of love's sweet perfume
I carefully choose, the colors so grand
To brighten my world, as they rest in my hand

In this simple act, I find solace and peace
Honoring love's essence, finding release
For though we're apart, our paths have diverged
The tradition lives on, in a gesture, preserved

So here's to the flowers, that bridge the divide
A testament to love, where hearts once did reside
For in the blooms I hold, a connection remains
Love's legacy continues, as its beauty sustains

Every Friday, with petals in hand
I honor the past, and the love that once spanned
A tradition renewed, a bond that won't sever
For love lives on, in every flower, forever.

Friday flowers bloom
Tradition carries on strong
Love's scent lingers still.

Writing my Story

In the depths of despair, I felt confined
Too many battles, too many times
My heart shattered, my spirit worn
A soul in turmoil, weathered and torn

I yearned to surrender, to call it an end
To break free from a world I couldn't mend
But in the darkness, a spark did ignite
A glimmer of hope, a whisper of light

Slowly, surely, I started to see
That life is much more, it holds the key
To rise from the ashes, to fight my own fight
To embrace the day, to bask in its light

Though the road was steep, and courage did wane
I discovered a strength that I could regain
With each scar and heartbreak, I found my voice
To stand tall again, to make my choice

I'll rewrite the story, I'll craft my tale
No longer defeated, no longer frail
In the face of adversity, I'll take my stand
To reclaim my power, to seize life's hand

No longer a victim, I'll become the guide
To navigate hardships, with strength as my guide
I'll dance to my rhythm, my dreams I'll pursue
For life is a canvas, and I'll paint it anew

Through valleys and mountains, I'll forge my own way
Embracing the struggle, come what may
For life is a symphony, and I'll sing the song
Of resilience and hope, where I belong

So let the battles come, and heartbreaks too
I'll rise, I'll fight, and I'll see it through
For within my spirit, there's a fire that burns
That life's pain also earns

I'll savor each moment, with all that I've got
And find my purpose, like a warrior sought
With the wisdom of scars and the strength to endure
I'll choose to live life, with a heart that's pure.

In shattered pieces
Love's kaleidoscope of pain
Rebuilding begins.

Whispers in the Night

In the stillness of night, secrets are told
In whispers that only the heart can hold
Unspoken dreams and desires take flight
In the sanctuary of the heart's own light

A language of emotions, soft and pure
In whispers of the heart, we endure
The highs and lows, the joy and despair
A tender reminder that love is always there

Listen closely to the whispers of your heart
For they hold the wisdom of life's ancient art
In their gentle cadence, you'll find your way
Guided by love, come what may.

Fragile love's demise
Echoes of a shattered bond
Mending scars in time.

A Shakespeare's Tale

A Shakespeare's tale I have to tell
Of a man who knew the world so well
Of human nature, its light and dark
And how it shapes our fate and mark

In "Macbeth," we see ambition's price
A tragic hero's fatal vice
His thirst for power, his guilt and strife
His downfall, a warning of life

In "Hamlet," we see a prince so lost
His father's death, his mind exhaust
Betrayal and revenge, his only goal
His tale, a tragedy of the soul

"The Merchant of Venice," a play of hate
Shylock's demand, Antonio's fate
A tale of prejudice and greed
Of mercy, justice, and human need

And then there's "Romeo and Juliet"
A love so pure, their fate offset
Their passion strong, their families feuding
Their love, a tragedy, forever enduring

In each of his plays, Shakespeare shows
The human heart, its joys and woes
A mirror to life, a glimpse of truth
A timeless wisdom, for ageless youth.

Brushstrokes of Words

Amidst the creation of life's vast array
Brushstrokes of words come forth to play
In art and poetry, a fusion profound
A collection of emotions, dreams unbound

With each stroke of color, emotions bloom
In poetry's embrace, tales find room
A dance of words, a painter's embrace
In this fusion, emotions interlace

The artist's brush, a portal to the soul
As vivid emotions find their role
A painting's essence, a poem's might
Together they create an explosion bright

In the landscapes painted, poems reside
The beauty of art and words coincide
A symphony of colors, verses' grace
In this union, hearts find their space

The strokes of genius, the rhymes sublime
A treasure trove of visions, a wondrous chime
A canvas brought to life, emotions unwind
In this collection, heart and mind aligned

As pages turn, the colors blend
In poetry the world transcends
A masterpiece of art, a soulful rhyme
In brushstrokes of works, a timeless prime

From dawn to dusk, the verses flow
In every stroke, the stories grow.

Shattered love's embrace
Tears rain on a broken heart
Healing whispers start.

Fluttering through the air with grace
A symbol of transformation and embrace
The butterfly, a creature of wonder
Reflects the beauty that we all ponder.

The Change

In a quiet corner, a cocoon hangs still
A shelter for a life that's yet to spill
Inside, a caterpillar's work is done
Its metamorphosis has just begun

The body starts to change, cell by cell
A transformation we know so well
What once was crawling, now it will fly
A butterfly will emerge, in the skye

Days and weeks pass, and the cocoon's shell
Begins to crack, revealing what will excel
A delicate creature, with wings and color
The butterfly is born, a true wonder

So too, our lives are like this cocoon
Our transformations, happening soon
We shed our old skin, and make way for new
Our own metamorphosis, we go through

And just like the butterfly, we can emerge
Stronger, freer, and able to surge, Into a life
of beauty, grace, and light.

The butterfly's colors and patterns
A symbol of life's diverse lanterns
Each unique, yet all beautiful in their own right
A reflection of the world's colorful light.

Let the butterfly inspire
As we navigate life's daunting wire
A symbol of hope, growth, and love
Guiding us to embrace the beauty above
The butterfly's print is a delicate thing
A symbol of transformation taking wing
From the caterpillar's crawl to the butterfly's flight
The transformation is a wondrous sight.

Art can inspire poetry, and poetry can inspire art.
With heartfelt thanks,

Tania.

About the Author

Tania Winther is a multidisciplinary artist, designer, poet and world citizen.

She has been greatly influenced by her wide and diverse background in both the sciences and the arts, and this comes to surface in her creative expression.

Through the interplay of words and visual art, I try to capture a broad spectrum of emotions, inviting readers and viewers to experience my creations on their own terms. This poetry collection represents a compilation of my poems written over the years, expressing my healing process through life stories, heartache and loss.

'Art can inspire poetry, and poetry can inspire art'.

ISBN 979-8-88940-704-1